TECH bytes

Self-Driving Car

by Stephen Currie

NORWOOD HOUSE PRESS

Cover: The interior of the self-driving car "Budii," that was manufactured by Rinspeed.

Norwood House Press
P.O. Box 316598
Chicago, Illinois 60631

For information regarding Norwood House Press, please visit our website at:
www.norwoodhousepress.com or call 866-565-2900.

Hardcover ISBN: 978-1-59953-762-7
Paperback ISBN: 978-1-60357-870-7

LIBRARY OF CONGRESS CATALOGING-IN-PUBLICATION DATA

Names: Currie, Stephen, 1960- author.
Title: Self-driving car / by Stephen Currie.
Description: Chicago, Illinois : Norwood House Press, [2016] | Series: Tech bytes | Includes bibliographical references and index. | Audience: 8-12.

| Audience: 4-6.
Identifiers: LCCN 2015027488| ISBN 9781599537627 (library edition : alk. paper) | ISBN 9781603578752 (ebook)
Subjects: LCSH: Autonomous vehicles--Juvenile literature. | Automobile industry and trade--Technological innovations--Juvenile literature. | Automobiles--Design and construction--Juvenile literature.
Classification: LCC TL152.8 .C87 2016 | DDC 629.2220285--dc23
LC record available at http://lccn.loc.gov/2015027488

313R—012018
Manufactured in the United States of America in North Mankato, Minnesota.

CONTENTS

Note: Words that are **bolded** in the text are defined in the glossary.

CHAPTER 1

Let the Car Do the Driving!

A car pulls up to a red light in a big city, slowing and then stopping like all the other cars around it. When the light turns green, the car **accelerates** until it reaches a normal speed. A block later, the car moves into the left lane, signals for a turn, and rounds the corner onto another street. Within a few minutes, the car pulls into a lot at an apartment complex and steers smoothly into a parking space. It is home but no one gets out. In fact, there is no one behind the wheel!

This vehicle is no ordinary vehicle. It may look like any other car on the road, but it has no driver. It is known as a self-driving, or driverless, car. (These cars are also known as autonomous vehicles. The word *autonomous* means "by itself.") This car works thanks to cameras, computers, and other technologies. It can roam the city streets without running into anything or causing an accident.

A car without a driver may sound impossible, but it is far from a fantasy.

Google was one of the first to begin perfecting a self-driving car.

Every month, inventors and engineers bring us closer to a time when driverless cars may be everywhere!

The Problem

Driverless cars make good sense for many reasons. First, for most people, autonomous vehicles would be more convenient than regular cars. Today, drivers must constantly watch the road or risk causing an accident. Only the passengers can safely read, write, or text as the car moves along, but in a self-driving car everyone is a passenger.

Anyone in the car can play video games, sleep, or surf the Internet. The ride will be more fun for everyone.

Second, driverless cars would make it easier for many people to travel on their own. Today people who are blind, for instance, cannot drive a car, but they could travel alone in a self-driving car. Chris Urmson works for the technology company Google. He notes that driverless cars would also help people who have physical difficulty driving. Even a child could ride in a driverless car without an adult present. In fact, self-driving cars might be a great way to bring children to school, camp, or a friend's house. This would save families time and energy.

A third advantage to driverless cars has to do with traffic. Today many highways and streets are near their full **capacity** many times a day. Because these roads are so full, cars and trucks move very slowly on them. Engineers say that driverless cars could increase the number of vehicles that can fit on one road at the same time. One expert says that because they can travel at a consistent speed, we might be able to fit eight or nine times as many cars on a road as we can today!

Safety First

The most important reason for driverless cars is safety. Cars are heavy, and they are powerful. Unfortunately, people often crash them. Because cars move at high speeds, those crashes can be tragic. Each year hundreds of thousands of people in the United States are **injured** in car accidents. More than 30,000 are killed. Worldwide more than 1 million people die in car crashes every year.

Sometimes poor roads are the cause of these accidents. Sometimes the main issue is bad weather. Sometimes a flat tire

With thousands of accidents happening daily, the hope is that self-driving cars will help cut down on or eventually eliminate all accidents.

or some other problem with the car is the cause. But the most common reason for a crash has to do with the driver. Drivers can be tired, angry, on drugs or alcohol, or not paying close attention to the road. Any of these states of mind can lead to an accident and even a death.

That is not the case with a driverless car. Autonomous vehicles cannot grow angry or tired. They cannot drink too much alcohol or take drugs. They never shift their attention from the road. Experts say that if everyone had a self-driving car, the number of car crashes would be much, much lower than it is today. Some think that the number of people killed in accidents would be very close to zero!

Elon Musk runs a car company called Tesla Motors. He says that regular driving

Elon Musk

Elon Musk is one of the people most involved in driverless cars. Musk was born in South Africa in 1971. He studied science and economics in college. He is best known as a business leader. He has founded companies that focus on software, solar power, and space exploration.

In 2004 Musk joined Tesla Motors, a carmaker that had been founded one year earlier. There Musk helped produce electric cars. He also worked on autonomous vehicles. He continues to look for ways to be an innovator—a person who does and tries new things.

is so dangerous that it should probably be illegal. As a result, he thinks that all regular vehicles should be replaced with self-driving cars.

Early Ideas

The idea of a driverless car dates back many years. At first it was only a fantasy—an idea about what the future might be like. In the 1950s, for instance, the Walt Disney film company made a movie called *Magic Highway USA*. It showed cartoon cars driving by themselves along the highway. The film predicted that at

The idea of a driverless car dates back many years, starting in the 1950s.

DID YOU KNOW?

The three most common causes of car accidents today are distracted driving, speeding, and drunk driving. All of these involve the driver rather than the car.

some point in the future, cars really would travel that way.

Little by little, people began to build cars that could do some self-driving. In 1962, for instance, a researcher named Robert Fenton built a car that did not need a driver. Most of the inside of the car was filled with electronics. This equipment was used to guide the car along a track that had an electric wire in the middle.

Fenton's car could go about 80 miles an hour—but only on the special track.

In the next decades, scientists continued to work on driverless cars. In the 1980s, for instance, a group of German scientists built a vehicle that used a camera and a tracking system to tell where the lanes of a highway were. This car could drive on its own. It could stay in its lane even if the lane curved. In 1995 researchers in Pittsburgh took another vehicle on a trip across the United States. Although traffic laws required drivers to operate the brakes and the gas pedal, the vehicle steered itself.

Even in 1995, technology was not good enough to build a car that would truly be able to drive on its own. Self-driving cars rely on computers to tell them where to go and how fast to drive. Unfortunately, the computers of this time were not powerful enough to do those things. Maps were also an issue. Driverless cars need very detailed maps, but unfortunately that kind of detail did not exist during the 1990s.

Cameras were a third issue. A driverless car uses dozens of tiny cameras to help it **navigate**. The cameras of the 1990s were too big and too costly to be used in this way.

Recent developments have reduced the size and cost of cameras needed for self-driving cars.

The 2000s

By the early 2000s, things were starting to change. Computers were smaller and cheaper. Maps and cameras were better. The US government encouraged companies to try building autonomous vehicles. In 2004 and 2005 one government **agency** sponsored a contest in which simple self-driving cars raced each other across the Mojave Desert in California. In 2004 none of the cars finished the 150-mile (241 km) race. None even came close. But in 2005 five vehicles finished the course. It included tight turns, narrow roads, and three tunnels.

The 2007 Urban Challenge

The two driverless car races in the Mojave Desert were sponsored by DARPA. This is a government agency. In 2007 DARPA sponsored another race for self-driving cars. This time it held the race in an **urban** area. The cars had to obey all the local traffic rules while completing a 60-mile (97 km) course in less than six hours.

More than a dozen teams entered the race, and six teams finished the course. The winning team was made up of engineers from Carnegie Mellon University in Pittsburgh. They had modified a Chevrolet Tahoe to drive on its own.

Self-driving cars prepare for DARPA's Urban Challenge in Victorville, California in 2007.

There were still big problems with the driverless cars of the early 2000s. Sometimes they went too fast or too slow. At other times they hit **obstacles** along their way or got stuck in the desert sand. The brakes on some of the cars did not work right. In 2004 one car managed to flip upside down before the race even started. Still, the designers of these cars had done amazing work. Just ten years earlier it would have been impossible to build cars that could take part in a race like that at all. Driverless cars were becoming a reality.

DID YOU KNOW? ?

The Mojave Desert is the site for many off-road races, including the self-driving challenges of 2004 and 2005. It has been the site of many airplane races as well.

CHAPTER 2

Self-Parking and Other Features

The companies that build driverless cars have different ideas about how the cars might look and how they might work. They also have different ideas about just how "driverless" the cars will be. Google, for instance, is hoping to have all cars be fully driverless by the early 2020s.

Some other companies are aiming instead for what they call "semiautonomous" cars. These cars would combine some features of driverless cars with those of cars that have human drivers. For these companies, the goal is not to have fully self-driving cars right away. Instead, they would slowly replace drivers with computers, one step at a time.

Semiautonomous Cars

The semiautonomous approach makes sense to these companies for many reasons. First, most states do not yet allow driverless cars, and it is not clear when they will change their laws to permit them. As of late 2015, just four states had allowed driverless vehicles on their roads.

Until all states permit self-driving cars, a fully autonomous vehicle will not be as useful as a car that can also be driven by an actual person.

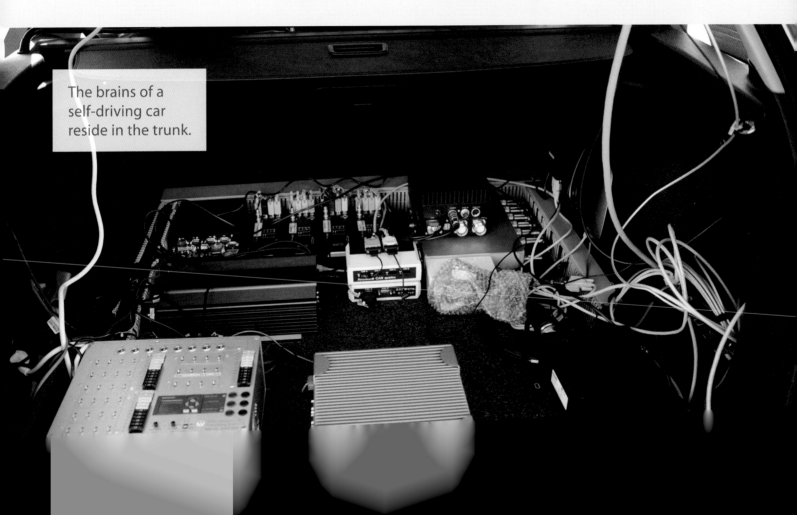

The brains of a self-driving car reside in the trunk.

Second, it will take time for drivers to become used to not being in control of their cars. Some people do not trust the computers, cameras, and maps in a driverless car to keep them safe. They fear that a self-driving car might **malfunction**. It might suddenly steer itself toward a highway overpass or another vehicle.

Third, many people do not see driving as a chore. Just the opposite—they enjoy driving very much. They are proud of their ability to drive. They like the feeling of rounding curves, changing lanes, and operating the vehicle safely. Author Nicholas Carr says that many people feel a sense of "flow" when they drive. This means that they feel in charge, capable, and good about themselves.

For all these reasons, many people are reluctant to use a self-driving car. It may make sense to add features over time instead of all at once. That allows people the chance to get used to each new feature before asking them to stop driving altogether.

Self-Parking

Many of these features are now available in regular cars. One example is auto-parking. A car that has auto-parking

A driver swipes his finger across an iPhone to initiate a self-parking demonstration at a car show in Las Vegas.

can drive itself into a parking spot. This feature was first developed as early as 1992. It was not put in cars available for purchase in the United States until 2007, and even then it was only an optional feature on some cars made by Lexus.

Auto-parking is used especially in parallel parking. This is common on streets in urban areas. In parallel parking, a car must often wedge itself along a curb between two other cars. That often involves moving the vehicle back and

Auto-parking

Self-parking cars were introduced to the United States in 2007, and they created a lot of buzz. In January of that year, for instance, TV host Oprah Winfrey spent part of one show discussing cars that could park themselves. Newspapers and magazines like the *New York Times* and the *Washington Post* published stories about the new feature, too.

Some people back then said that the technology did not work as well as it should. It was hard to park on hills, for instance. Many people saw that auto-parking would quickly improve and a few understood that it might someday lead to truly driverless cars.

An automatic parking distance sensor is located on the dashboard of a self-driving car.

forth, changing the position of the wheels each time. This can be hard even for experienced drivers to do, especially if the space is small. It blocks traffic and takes time. It can lead to dents and scratches on the car that is being parked—and on the cars around it.

A self-parking system changes all that. The driver does not maneuver the car into the parking space. Instead, he or she pushes a button to get a computer to move the car. The computer is helped in this task by sensors or cameras. These devices determine the position of curbs, driveways, and other vehicles. Then they send the information to the computer. The computer analyzes the data. Then it moves the steering wheel to the correct angle to guide the car into the space.

DID YOU KNOW? ?

Most self-driving cars can be operated by a person in an emergency. For instance, some have brake pedals that can be pressed to force the car to stop.

The driver does have two responsibilities while this is going on. First, he or she must shift the car between forward and reverse when told (usually by a computerized voice). Drivers must also hold and release the brake pedal when the computer says to do so. Ultimately, self-parking is not yet fully autonomous, but these responsibilities are small and the computer does the main work.

Google designed its first self-driving car to look friendly and non-threatening. The goal is to get people to think the cars are cute rather than possibly dangerous.

At first, auto-parking was only available in costly cars, but it proved to be a popular feature. Researchers continued to work on it, and they found ways to make it cost less and less. Today auto-parking is included on many less costly cars. As people use this feature, they will become more willing to allow computers and cameras to help them with their driving. In this way, auto-parking is one step on the path to a fully self-driving car.

Automatic Cruise Control

Cruise control is another form of automatic driving. It has been available in cars since the 1970s. With cruise control, drivers reach a chosen speed in a vehicle. Then they press a button to engage the control. Drivers can take their foot off the gas pedal, and the car will then keep going at that speed. The engine automatically slows the vehicle when it goes downhill and increases power as it goes uphill. Today most cars sold have cruise control as a standard feature.

Cruise control is not perfect. The driver needs to be alert to the presence of other vehicles. If the car approaches

A driver engages the cruise control.

a slow-moving truck, the driver must remove the cruise control or risk a crash. The driver must tap the brake or push the button again to take control of the car's speed before disaster strikes. In this way cruise control is not fully automatic, but that is changing.

Some new cars today are being sold with so-called autonomous cruise control. Cars with this feature use sensors to help them tell where other vehicles are on the road. When the car goes near another vehicle or another vehicle comes near it from behind, the sensors then tell a computer what

Developing Autonomous Cruise Control

Different car companies have built cruise controls that work automatically. The first was a company called Mitsubishi. This car maker is in Japan. It made an automatic cruise control system in 1992. Toyota, which is also a Japanese company, built a better system in 1997.

Two years after that, the Mercedes company in Germany built an improved cruise control system. Since then, BMW, Jaguar, and Lexus car companies have worked to improve the system as well. Because of all these companies, autonomous cruise control is something that works well today!

is going on. The computer then adjusts the car's speed to make sure it avoids a crash.

Autonomous cruise control does not make a vehicle self-driving, but it is a change that moves cars in that direction. As drivers get more used to letting the car do the work, they will see the benefits of other self-driving features and they will become more willing to consider using a fully autonomous car when one becomes available.

Auto-braking

A third automatic feature that more and more cars have is called auto-braking.

This is a system that lets cars stop by themselves. Sensors detect the presence of an obstacle in the road. This could be another car, a lane blocked by road construction, or a large animal. The sensors then alert an onboard computer.

What happens then depends on the system. Some of these systems quickly alert the driver that there might be a problem. This may be through flashing lights, a voice command, or both. It is then up to the driver to apply the brakes if he or she thinks this is needed.

Other systems apply the brakes automatically. In this case the driver does not have to react at all. The only risk is that the sensors might detect something that is not actually a **hazard**. The sensors may then cause a crash by stopping the car when other drivers do not expect it.

Auto-braking is less common on today's cars than self-parking and autonomous cruise control, but it has the same basic effect. All three systems make cars more automated. All three reduce the role of the driver in operating the vehicle. All three make driving safer, and all three may make it easier for drivers of the future to accept a fully self-driving car.

CHAPTER 3

On the Road to a Self-Driving Car?

Since 2010 many companies have worked hard to build and design driverless cars. Google is one. Tesla is another. So is a company called Delphi Automotive. Many traditional carmakers are starting to make self-driving cars as well. These include Ford, Mercedes, and General Motors.

These companies all have different ideas of what a driverless car should look like, and no two use exactly the same technologies. Still, they all have some important ideas in common, and they are all working to develop products that will travel smoothly and safely on the roads of the world.

Outside and In

From the outside, a driverless car looks like a regular car. There is a good reason for that. Most self-driving cars today are regular cars that have been **transformed**

Delphi Automotive showcases their driverless Audi Q5 sport-utility vehicle.

on the inside. In 2015, for instance, Delphi built a self-driving car. It was originally an Audi sport-utility vehicle. At some point, companies may make changes to the way the outside of a self-driving car looks. For now they are focusing on the technology that lets the car move by itself. Most of these companies have spent little time or money on the outside of self-driving cars.

Right now much of the inside of self-driving cars looks familiar, too. Driverless cars will still carry passengers so they will still need seats, seat belts, and cup holders. Self-driving cars do not really need brake pedals, gas pedals, and a steering wheel, but they will likely be made with these features for some time to come. That is because most laws do not yet permit driverless cars to operate unless there is a person in the front seat who can take over in case of an emergency.

Computers, Sensors, and Cameras

A self-driving car is very different from a regular car in many other ways. A driverless car is like a giant computer with wheels. It may have 30 or more cameras. The car is constantly using sensors, or technologies that look for information in the world around the car.

Lane markings are a good example. A camera takes pictures of the lane markers on a street or a highway as the car moves along. The pictures are sent to a computer on board the vehicle. The computer analyzes the pictures. Is the car too close to one of the lane markers? Is it too far away from another? If the vehicle is even slightly off course, the computer will make a correction. It will shift the angle of the wheels so the car is going down the middle of the lane. At the same time, other cameras may be scanning the road ahead and the road behind to give the computers information about what else is going on nearby.

Self-driving cars use more than just cameras to gather information. Many of

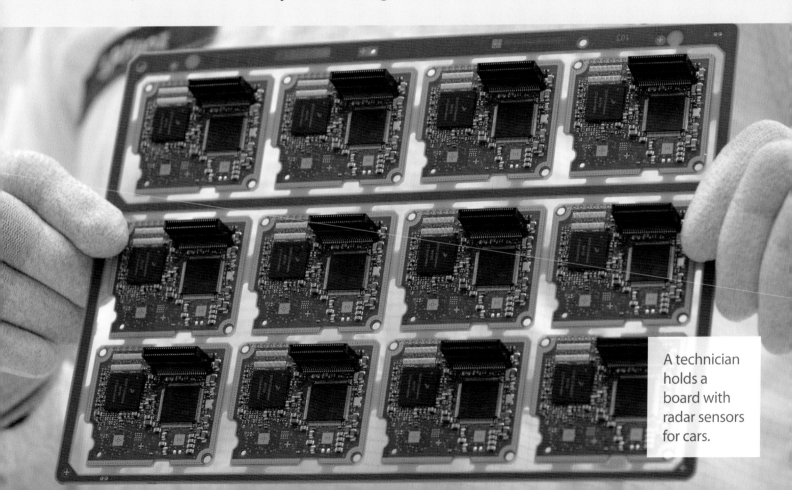

A technician holds a board with radar sensors for cars.

Early Laws

In 2011 Nevada became the first state to let autonomous cars drive on public roads. It was also the first place in the world to do so. Part of the reason Nevada passed this law was because of Google. Google wanted to test its driverless cars on public roads, and company officials liked the long empty highways that cross the state. Nevada required that these cars have passengers while they are being driven, just in case something goes wrong.

Two of the next few states to pass laws that allow self-driving cars also had connections to the auto and engineering industries. These were Michigan and California. Both are home to car companies such as Ford and Tesla. California is home to many engineering firms. Other states may soon pass such laws as well.

them also use **radar**. *Radar* is short for "radio detection and ranging." It involves sending out radio waves. These bounce off objects and return to the sender. Computers measure how long it takes for the waves to return. Then they can tell how close an object is. Radar helps determine how far away other vehicles are from a driverless car. The onboard computers analyze the information from radar. Then they guide the car around or away from these obstacles.

More Sensors

Other types of sensors are important as well. One big problem with driverless cars has to do with **pedestrians**. Radar is good at finding solid objects made of metal, such as other cars. But it is not very good at finding people, so some driverless cars have **infrared** sensors. These allow the cars to find pedestrians, especially at night.

Infrared uses light waves that cannot be seen by the human eye. Most objects put out infrared light. The sensors can pick up this light even if a person cannot. If a sensor detects the presence of a person on the road, then the computer takes over and guides the vehicle to slow down, stop, or swerve so it will not collide with the pedestrian.

Another common type of sensor is called an **ultrasonic** sensor. It sends out sound waves. The human ear cannot hear these sound waves, but they are very helpful when a driverless car is backing up or trying to park. The ultrasonic waves bounce off other vehicles or obstacles. This lets the computers analyze whether the car has enough space to back up safely—or to park in that spot.

DID YOU KNOW? ?

A self-parking car does not rely on just one sensor to help the vehicle park safely. Instead, it relies on a whole "suite" of sensors—usually more than a dozen.

More Equipment

Driverless cars also make use of other equipment. The onboard computers must always be able to tell exactly where the car is, so a GPS is needed. A GPS uses signals bounced off of satellites that **orbit** the Earth. These signals can let the computers know just where the car is.

Maps are important, too. The computers in a driverless car can access maps of all the

Sophisticated computers with detailed maps help direct driverless cars.

roads the car might drive on. These maps have a lot of detail. They may even include curbs, stoplights, and road signs. As the car drives along, the maps are automatically updated. For instance, if an image from a camera does not show a certain street sign that appears on the map, the computer may remove the sign from the map. It is even possible for a computer on a self-driving car to draw its own map as the car moves through an unfamiliar place.

Engineers are also working on ways to let driverless cars communicate with each other. Suppose that a self-driving car drives over an icy stretch of road. Its computers might send signals to other cars in the area. Those signals would tell the computers in those cars that there was ice and tell them its exact location. The other

cars' computers could then make sure the cars were going at a safe speed for the icy road. Communication like this could help reduce the number of accidents.

If self-driving cars can communicate, that could also lead to changes in the way streets are designed. Today stop signs and stoplights are needed to let drivers know when it is safe to go. With driverless cars on the road, that

GPS

The global positioning system (GPS) uses a network of satellites. These are human-made objects that move around the Earth. GPS lets people know exactly where they are at any given time. These systems are very useful in helping drivers plan routes. They can also help drivers avoid traffic. Bus and trucking companies use them to keep track of where their vehicles are, too.

A driver sets his car's GPS device.

Without a GPS, it would be very hard to build a driverless car. There is no driver in a self-driving car so the GPS must direct the vehicle along the correct routes. If it were not for GPS technology, autonomous vehicles would probably not exist.

may change. There may not need to be any traffic signals at all. The computers on each car can consult and decide which will go first, second, and so on.

Progress

These **innovations** have not yet been perfected. For instance, some of the systems do not work as well on cloudy

A driverless car competes in the 2004 Mojave Desert race.

or rainy days as they do on clear days. GPS units are not always perfectly accurate. This can be a problem when a car is driving along a narrow road. Some of the cars do not react correctly when something unexpected happens, such as a deer jumping out into the middle of the road, and the cost of all these sensors and gadgets is very high. It is not clear when self-driving cars will become cheap enough for most people.

Still, engineers are making a lot of progress. As recently as 2004, not a single driverless car could complete a 150-mile (241 km) race in the Mojave Desert. Today driverless cars have traveled hundreds of thousands of miles. Nearly all of these miles have been without accidents and many of these miles have been alongside other cars on the streets and highways of states like California and Michigan. Driverless cars are closer and closer to becoming a common sight on roads in the U.S. and all over the world!

CHAPTER 4

Looking to the Future

Most of the people who design and build self-driving cars today say that these cars are the wave of the future. Elon Musk of Tesla, for instance, says that driverless cars will be everywhere before long. Many engineers who are working on self-driving cars for Google and other companies agree. To them the advantages of driverless cars are so great that it makes no sense to keep using regular cars.

If driverless cars become common, they will surely change the world in dozens of ways, large and small. The lives of adults and children alike could be changed. So could businesses from shopping malls to insurance companies. These changes may be positive or negative. Musk and others say they will be positive, but not everyone is so sure.

Major Changes

All experts agree that self-driving cars will bring about many important changes. One of these involves transportation for people who cannot or do not drive, such as blind

Elon Musk of Tesla believes that driverless cars will be everywhere before long.

people. For many years the blind have needed buses, taxis, or friends with cars if they wanted to make a trip. With driverless cars, blind people can have their own transportation.

Car accidents would become a thing of the past if people moved to self-driving cars, too. Even with seat belts, air bags, and other features meant to improve safety, cars still are dangerous. No matter how careful a driver is, he or she is in jeopardy. This is because there may be less cautious drivers who are also on the road. Self-driving cars would make accident rates drop sharply and that would be a great thing.

Parking would be very different as well. Drivers like to park their cars as close to the entrances of stores as possible. That saves them from having to walk long distances, especially in bad weather. A driverless car could drop all the passengers off at the front entrance. Then it could go a much greater distance to park—even a mile or more.

Once the car was parked, it would wait for a signal to come back and pick up the passengers. In a world of driverless cars,

A driving instructor helps a legally blind man operate a self driving car.

Laws and Vehicles

One of the big issues with driverless cars has to do with the law. Governments are working on making new laws that will address self-driving vehicles, but not all governments have passed the same laws. The exact laws make a big difference in how quickly driverless cars will catch on.

For instance, states will need to decide whether self-driving cars can go on the road without a person inside. If states choose to allow this, then families may find it easy to get along with just one car. The car can drop one person at work or school. Then it can return for another person, and so on. But, if states choose to require a person in every self-driving vehicle, it will be much harder for families to manage with just a single car.

stores would not need to have their own parking lots. People would no longer need to circle the lots again and again, wasting time and gas in order to look for a good parking spot.

Some Possible Changes

Other changes are less certain. Some people, for instance, say that moving

DID YOU KNOW? ?

In 2012 Google filmed a legally blind man, Steve Mahan, behind the wheel of a driverless car. Google then posted the video on YouTube.

to self-driving cars will mean that there will be more cars on the road. They point out that people who cannot drive regular cars will benefit from owning driverless cars. They also say that families that already own two cars might want a third or even a fourth car. An extra car might be ideal for taking children places, for instance.

Other people think that driverless cars will do the opposite. They will reduce the number of cars people own. A married couple that currently has two cars, for example, might be able to share one car if that car did not need a driver. The car could drop the wife at work at 8:00 a.m., for instance, then return home and take the husband to work an hour later. Then later in the day the car could bring both of them home as well.

Sharing cars might not be limited to people who live together. Friends or neighbors might realize that they could manage with just one car between them, too. As experts see it, driverless cars will make the roads less **congested**. That would save fuel and money. It would also make traveling a more pleasant experience.

Experts say driverless cars will make the roads less congested.

Cities and Suburbs

Another possible change involves where people choose to live. Some experts say that self-driving cars will encourage people to make their homes in cities. Today many people do not want to live in cities. Part of the reason is that city traffic is often very bad and it can take a long time for city dwellers to go anywhere. If there are fewer cars on the streets, that could make urban life more appealing to many people.

Hacking

One concern about self-driving cars is hacking. In hacking, people gain unlawful access to a computer system. For driverless cars, the worry is that people might use computers or cell phones to change the car's programming. That could prove to be very dangerous!

Say a hacker gains control of a car's computers. He or she could reprogram them to cause a crash, such as by steering directly into a pole, stopping abruptly in the middle of a street, or preventing the brakes from working. Governments are aware of the possible problems and so are carmakers. Solutions to these problems are still being considered.

Again, some experts hold the opposite opinion. They think that driverless cars will make people want to live farther away from where they work and shop. Travel would be much easier with an autonomous vehicle. People who once had to drive can sleep, eat, or read in a driverless car. People who live an hour or more from their jobs would enjoy the **commute** much more than they would if they had to drive. These experts say that self-driving cars will make more people move to the suburbs.

More Questions

Self-driving cars may lead to other changes, too. When two cars with drivers collide, the insurance companies usually

Self-driving cars will allow drivers to make better use of the time spent commuting to and from work.

problem was. Maybe the problem was with the computer in one of the cars. Then the company that made the computer might be at fault. Or perhaps the problem had to do with the maps that tell the car where to go. Then the mapmakers might be to blame. Self-driving cars could certainly change the way insurance companies do business!

One final question involves free time. Some experts say that driverless cars will make life much easier for people. After all, everyone will be a passenger, and no one will need to do the driving! All that time that drivers would normally spend focusing on the road could be used for fun activities like reading, doing crossword puzzles, and talking to friends.

pay for the damage to the cars along with any medical bills for the drivers or passengers. The insurance company that pays the most is the one that insures the driver who is more to blame.

What happens when two driverless cars collide? Who is more to blame then? The insurance company has to figure out which car had the problem—and what the

Others are skeptical. Many new technological changes were supposed to give people more spare time, but they did not. Instead of relaxing while the washing machine washed the clothes, for instance, people tended to find new tasks and responsibilities. Many experts think that people will simply find more jobs to do in the time they used to spend driving. We may find out very soon who is right!

accelerates [ack-SELL-uh-rates]: Speeds up; goes faster.

agency [A-jen-see]: An office or department.

capacity [cuh-PAH-si-tee]: The largest number or amount that will fit.

commute [cuh-MUTE]: A trip to and from work.

congested [cun-JES-ted]: Full, especially with vehicles or people.

hazard [HAZ-erd]: Danger.

infrared [in-fruh-RED]: A type of light not visible to humans.

injured [IN-jerd]: Hurt, especially in an accident.

innovations [in-no-VAY-shuns]: Ideas and creations that are new.

malfunction [mal-FUNK-shun]: A breakdown or failure in a machine.

navigate [NAV-uh-gate]: To make one's way, especially in an unfamiliar place.

obstacles [OB-stuh-kuls]: Objects in the path of a person or thing.

orbit [OR-bit]: To circle something else, such as a star or planet.

pedestrians [puh-DES-tree-uns]: People who walk outdoors.

radar [RAY-dar]: Radio waves used to tell how far away an object is.

transformed [trans-FORMED]: Made to look or act very different.

ultrasonic [ul-tra-SAH-nick]: Sounds that cannot be heard by the human ear.

urban [ER-bun]: Having to do with a city.

FOR MORE INFORMATION

Books

Katie Marsico, *Self-driving Cars*. New York: Children's Press, 2016.

Peter C. Wayner, *Future Ride: 80 Ways the Self-Driving, Autonomous Car Will Change Everything*. www.Createspace.com, 2013.

Internet Sources

Doug Aamodt and Corey Protin, "Driverless Cars Are Coming," http://time.com/90385/driverless-cars.

Council on Foreign Relations, "Driverless Cars," www.cfr.org/technology-and-science/driverless-cars/p32734.

Ben Geier, "Driverless Cars Could Mean Fewer Cars on the Road," fortune.com/2015/02/09/driverless-car-study.

Jemima Kiss, "Self-driving Cars: Safe, Reliable—But a Challenging Sell for Google." *The Guardian*, October 6, 2015, http://www.theguardian.com/technology/2015/oct/06/google-self-driving-car-jemima-kiss.

John Patrick Pullen, "You Asked: How Do Driverless Cars Work?," http://time.com/3719270/you-asked-how-do-driverless-cars-work.

Ritkia Shah, "Are Self-driving Cars Closer Than We Think?," *CNBC*, October 14, 2015, http://www.cnbc.com/2015/10/14/self-driving-cars-closer-than-we-think-expert.html.

Bruce Upbin, "Let's Go for a Ride in Traffic with Audi's Self-Driving Car," *Forbes*, January 8, 2014, http://www.forbes.com/sites/bruceupbin/2014/01/08/lets-go-for-a-ride-in-traffic-with-audis-self-driving-car-video/.

Bill Whitaker, "Hands off the Wheel," *CBS News*, October 4, 2015, http://www.cbsnews.com/news/self-driving-cars-google-mercedes-benz-60-minutes/.

INDEX

A

Accidents
assessing blame for, 42
deaths/injuries from, 6, 7
leading causes of, 7–8, 10
self-driving cars could
eliminate, 8, 35
Auto-braking, 22–23
Auto-parking (self-parking),
16–20, 29

C

Cameras, 11
Carr, Nicholas, 16
Commuting, 40, 42
Cruise control, 20–22

D

DARPA, 12

F

Fenton, Robert, 10

G

GPS (global positioning system),
30, 32, 33

H

Hacking, 40

I

Insurance, 42

L

Laws/legal issues, 14–15, 28, 37

M

Magic Highway USA (film),
9–10

Mahan, Steve, 37
Maps, 11, 30–31, 42
Mitsubishi, 22
Mojave Desert, 11–13, 33
Musk, Elon, 8–9, 34, 35

R

Radar, 27–28

S

Self-driving cars
advantages of, 6–7
communication between,
31–32
drawbacks to, 14–16
early work on, 9–11
hacking of, 40
impact on where people
choose to live, 39–40

Stephen Currie has written dozens of books for young people, along with teacher guides, textbook chapters, and other educational materials. He has also taught at levels ranging from kindergarten to college. He lives in the Hudson Valley region of New York State.